You can be a
business Owner

21 Awesome Home Based Businesses

*Take a Chance
on You*

Look beyond Obstacles

DON'T SAY WHAT YOU CAN'T DO.
KNOW WHAT YOU CAN DO AND MOVE FROM THERE.

A dream is only a dream if you don't do something about it.

We must step out on faith if we intend on making something good happen.

You say you want to be a business owner but don't have any money.

As you read this booklet you will find it don't take much to start.

Can they be trusted?

Be careful with your money and ideas..........

It's sadden me to say, but there are many people out here who prey on people that are looking to start their own business, but don't have all the know how. No one have all the answers. I ask that you be very careful as to whom you are giving all your information to. Be careful of who you allow to take part in your business adventure.

People will charge you a great deal of money to do things that you yourself can do for little to no money at all. Example: I ran into a guy that advertised getting you a tax ID number for your business for $250. A tax ID number is free. All you have to do is go the IRS website, www.irs.gov. You have the options to do your application on line, fax or send it via mail.

Don't get me wrong that is his business but why do we have to be like that? I myself have charged a $25 fee to do a tax ID form. $250 that is way too much, but if you don't know and you need that to open your bank account, then what do you do?

Another example, I talked to a lady about starting a program in her establishment to help the people that she was servicing. I set up a meeting and went in to her office all professional. I had my presentation flawless. She then told me that she would get back to me and five months later I saw this lady on the early morning news with her idea to offer my services to clients not only in her place of business but in others that do what she did. I was like oh wow. She had everything that I presented to her from the kinds of service, how they would be offered, to the people I would bring in to help out with the services.

So be careful, it's a dog eat dog world out here. There is nothing wrong with a little bit of competition and I welcome it. I believe that no one can do what I can do. They can change it, add to it or even take away from it, but I know that I can do it better. SO take that on with you as you begin to give birth to your new business.

I know you can do it. Go slow, take your time, ask questions, do your research.

Keep me posted on how things are going. You can always reach me at fitness4life3@yahoo.com

You can make it happen!

DO you have a Vision?

Letter from the Author

This booklet was made for those of you that have a vision but just don't know what to do with it. I have for a very long time dreamed of being my own boss. I would write things down and sometime even go as far as to get a Tax ID numbers for the business. Something in me would never let me go a step further. That thing was fear. I was afraid to step out. I was afraid that I would fail. The more I would sit down and think of businesses that I thought I would be good at or could make a profit from the more I would do nothing. I have tons of manuals, booklets, programs, business ideas written up and ready to put in action, but nope I did not believe in myself. I know I would not be able to pull it off. No matter what others would say I just could not do it.

One think I realized is that people can tell me all the motivational things they wanted but if I did not believe in myself nor had the faith that God would make away, I would never do anything. I had to reach deep inside and find that which was in me to make a stand for myself and make something happen.

In 2000 open my very first store which was a thrift shop for plus size woman. After only 7 months I was closed. I did not do my home work and had to close because I was not prepared. In 2008 I reopened my store and it lasted for one year. This time I did things a little bit better. I could not afford to open in my own location I subleased space in a friends business. This did not turn out to be the best thing for me or the business. Needless to say the more I try the more I learn and know how to do things better. So in 2010 I will reopen my shop once again with the knowledge that I have from my previous experiences.

So from me to you, just try it. Working from home will allow you to gain the knowledge that you need to go forward into your own location.

Don't keep allowing people to tell you what you can't do, just do what you can until you can do better. Start small and move form there.

Why work from home?

There are many reasons why someone would want to work from home. Studies shows that there are over 20 million home based business and about 70% are owned by woman. When you have a home to maintain, dinner, the children, laundry and all the many other duties that come with maintaining a home, you don't have many more hours in the day to go out and punch the clock.

This has lead woman (and men) to start working from home. The best way to start is by researching what is already working. If it has been done and seems to be working why not get your 15 minutes or more of fame with the same type of business. Mc Donald's is not the only burger joint that has made millions selling burgers and fries. Think about it if no one else would have thought about making cars Ford would be the only person to manufacture them.

You can also choose to go with your talents. There is something that you are good at. It can be as simple as baking a cake, or cooking a meal, this is your talent. Why not make some money of it? You might not know what your skill or talent is at this point but that is not a problem. Ask a friend or a family member what they think you are good at. If you agree try your hand at it. Make it your home business.

Home businesses are a great way to get in on the ground floor of your future endeavors because of the low overhead and no employees. One of the main things you must do is find a spot in your home and designate it only for your business. You can use your current home phone or purchase a inexpensive cell phone. You don't have to worry about rent you are already paying that. You don't have to worry about another gas or electric bill why because you are already paying that.

What I will suggest is that you get a computer, a fax, and a copier or a simple 3-in-1 machine that has it all. You can find one under $80 at your local Walmart or K-mart stores. Get a desk and chair and you are ready for work.

Please know I am not trying to make this out to be easy as 1 2 3 but you wont know if you don't try, just how easy it may be!

Start somewhere to get somewhere

No one person has all the answers.

All great businesses started somewhere.

In this booklet I have taken 21 businesses that can be awesome home bases businesses. You have the choice to take on one of these or do further research to see what else maybe out there.

There are many books you can purchase or take out of your local library to read about starting your very own business.   Many people think it is very costly to start a business. I say to them that if you don't try you will never know what your potential financial outcome can be. If you are not going to take the risk for yourself then I ask who will.

There are so many people that have started businesses right at home and had to move out because the outcome was go great. If you don't start somewhere you will never end up anywhere. It doesn't take much too just start. Just get your feet wet if you will. See what could happen. Go ahead. Take a chance on you and your future. If you are one of those people that don't like risk how will you know what your potential is?

When you are choosing a business make sure it is something that others can use. It can be a service or a product.   As you look out in your neighborhoods what do you see? There are many people that have taken the same chance that you are about to take. Let's look at McDonalds………….. One burger…. look at them now. Can you be as large as McDonalds, Burger King, Zale's or Little Debbie? Sure why not, they had to start somewhere.

You maybe thinking that they had money to invest. Well that may be true, but the point is they tried and look at them now!

Home based Business

If you think I am going to tell you that it will be a piece of cake to just start a home based business think again......I am not saying that at all. With anything you do it's going to take some time to see a profit. That is if you are working from home, an office or renting a building. You have to look into you local, state and government to see if there are any licenses, permits or rules and regulation needed for the business that you chose.

Make sure that you are doing all you need to do to be a legitimate business so that you wont get into any trouble with the laws of your state. There are many websites that you can go to and get information on starting businesses in your home town. If you can't find anything lookup your local Small Business Administration Office in the yellow pages and ask them for direction on your journey to a home based business.

The best advice I can give is research research research research. Lookup as much information as you can. Ask others in the same line of work. You will be surprised that some people are willing to share information but don't get discouraged if some people will not share information. Just move on and continue to look for all the help you can get.

RESEARCH   RESEARCH

RESEARCH   RESEARCH

Table of Contents

If you sow good seeds

You will reap a good harvest

Your home office

Time and space
You will need to find time daily to work on your home business if you want

to be successful. It is very important to have space only for your business.

This will cost you nothing.

Computer
A computer is great for keeping records. All the information about your
contacts and also to make your contracts and or service agreements

If you currently have one great if not you can start out with a refurbished
one. $200

Printer
The best printer you can use for your home business is a 3-n-1 with a

printer, copier and scanner. This will be a great asset to your business.

A new 3-n-1 will cost you less than $100 at your local Wal-mart or Office
supply store.

Telephone, Fax
This is one feature you can not do with out. If you already have a home

phone great. You can add another line just for your business.

This can be free or you can add a cell phone for as little as $40 a month.

Each home based business listed in this booklet are just suggestions. Take your talent and turn it into cash. It doesn't matter if someone else is doing it or not. Remember if it can be done then why can't you be the one doing it. Don't think for a minute that because its already being done there is no room for you.

You are never alone. You have friends and family members that will or can help you get started. If you don't shoot me an e-mail and we can chat it out. Friends call me Alicia e-mail address is fitness4life3@yahoo.com
You can even join or start a small business club for like minded people to share ideas and experiences.

Don't get frustrated and stay there. Any time you venture into new things it can become frustrating when things don't go the way you would like. Remember things that are worth it will take time to develop. When you feel yourself getting frustrated step back take some time away from your new idea and relax. Just remember to get back on it.

Don't give it away. Make sure you are pricing your items or services so that you can make a profit. Don't just give it away because you like what you are doing. The idea is to make some extra cash that you can use for recreation or even to help pay some bills. Don't over price but please don't under price.

Don't let your fear stop you from your dreams. Fear is a ugly thing that will keep you from stepping out on faith and believing that you can. Let me tell you…YOU CAN DO IT JUST GO AHEAD AND TRY. IF IT DON'T WORK THE 1ST TIME TRY IT AGAIN LATER. The idea is to find something that you like doing and will help you make some extra cash.

Research Research Research It is so important to do some research in the area you would like to venture. Talk to people that are currently in your line of work. Examine what they are doing and think of ways you can make it better. A little competition is a wonderful thing. Go head take your shot at it.

CHECK YOUR STATE LAWS Don't get caught with your pants down. Always check with your state laws about business start ups. If you are not going to do your business on a regular basis you may meet some special laws that you don't have to get any special license or permits. Call around and ask questions to cover you own butt.

Baby Steps are always good Take baby steps. Don't make this hard. Keep things as simple as possible. Make sure you are jotting down goals you need to get this new venture off the ground. Making goals are very important. Don't go to the next step or goal without fully completing the one before. Good luck keep me posted. Email me.

1. Alterations / Sewing

Who don't need to get hooked up? Now if you are one of the people that can work the needle and thread this is a sure fire thing for you. There are many guys that are shorter than average and would love to be able to have their pants hemmed. Don't forget about the people that are on the weight loss crave. They would love to have there clothing taken in to fit the new them. Replace zippers, add fabric all that stuff. You sew you know what to do.

Start-Up
What you already have.
Spend about $25 on needles and threads (ppsssstt dollar store)
Get in the free or low cost TV guides,
If you have a sawing machine great if not get a starter one from Walmart $90
Free make some calls to your friends and family and tell them to tell someone.
Ask if you can post in Church bulletins, on store boards, and in local restaurants.

Read up on current fashion trends if you are more in to doing actual designs. If this is something you know you could do go ahead take the chance. There is so much money to be made. People will come to you like flies to honey. Times are hard and people can't afford to buy new clothing they need you so get to work.

Suggestion:
Get some used clothing from the goodwill or local resale shop and put your own touch on them. Let your imagination run wild. Do about 5 to 10 items and then have a show and see what others have to say as you sale them all. Do this a few times or make this a part of your business. What do you have to lose……….. Let's SEE……….... nothing.

Alterations & Repairs

2. Bookkeeping

This would be a great at home business for you if you are good with numbers and record keeping. Target small businesses that can't afford to contract major accounting firms. Get you a nice contract together and begin to scout the neighborhood for small business that would like to get some professional help. Let them know your services would allow them to spend more time doing what they do, while you take care of business bookkeeping.

Start-Up
Computer you may already have or use the one at the local library   disk, 5 to start   3-in-1 copier, printer and fax, $75   business cards you can do on your own, temples $8 at Office Depot

To make sure you are up on current financial information and techniques take some at home or online classes to refresh your skills. Ask a friend to allow you to make them a budget. Begin small and work your way up to the larger task.

Suggestion:
Go to local small business and feel them out. Look around see how many customers they have in the time you are there. Make sure you get their address, and phone number. You can get this information off the internet or phone book. Do this with about 15 businesses to start. Design yourself a nice intro letter about yourself and what you can bring to their company. Make sure you let them know they need you. (In a professional manner) Mail them out and wait for the inquires to come in. If you don't hear from any of them after three weeks call and see if they received your letter. If any of these 15 doesn't need your services at this time don't worry just get another 15 and do the same thing.

3.   Candles

If you are a candle person you can surely welcome this fine art. Making them can be as easy as putting food in a container or as hard as trigonometry. There is money to be made here. People love the nice small of a burning fragrance candle. How about a nice relaxing bath with candle lite all around. Don't forget those of us that like aroma therapy candles. WOW Its up to you to sale pre-made candles or make them up yourself. It's always good to have your personal touch on what you sale.

Start-Up
 This really depends on what you plan to do. If you are going in from starch you will need material to start such as wax, wicks, molds and containers. These prices can vary store to store.

If you choose to sale per-made candles shop around over the internet and find wholesale companies that allow you to purchase small amounts of material to start. Some places may even have business start-up kits

Do research to make sure you can afford this at home business. Your start-up can be as small as $100 to $500.

Suggestion:
Buy some very inexpensive plain candles, some ribbons and bows, clear wrapping or tissue paper and go to town. Make something beautiful from something simple. Invite over some friends and family. Make sure you tell them to bring their pocket books. Have a few light snacks maybe give some inexpensive wine. Call it a treat your self to beauty gathering or something along that lines. Don't forget set your prices so that you can make a profit.

4.   Catering

Catering can be a wide range of things from a simple dinner for two to a large gathering for 100 plus. Some people love to throw parties but don't have the time to prepare the food and make the arrangement as well as conduct their everyday task. If you are a person that loves the kitchen this home base business can bring in a substantial income your way.

Start-Up
Because you are doing catering this will vary. Pots, pans, stove which you already have are your biggest purchases. You may need to get larger ones to handle larger orders. I say try searching your local thrift shops. You can find great things there.

Spices and ingredients will vary depending on your job. Just make sure you are current with rates before you quote a price to your client. You can also ask for a down payment before you begin to prepare any foods.

Suggestion:
Contact a few (about 25 to start) smaller schools, churches, wedding planners and night clubs. Mail out an invitation to sample your dishes. Choose a few simple things and a couple extravagant ones. Varity is the spice of life. When you contact these individuals make sure you get a confirmation as to if they are coming or not. This way you won't over spend.

Make sure you have some business cards and something that highlight your best dishes and contact information. Also have a sign in sheet for your guest so this way you can reach them at a later date. Name, phone, business and their title.

Don't forget friends and family is a great free way to advertise

5. Computer Training

New age, new technology. Almost everything you encounter these day have something to do with the computer. Many older people find that they can't do much as before without spending some time learning about the ways of modern times. Teaching someone how to use the basic functions associated with the computer can be and is a great way to make some extra cash. These services can be provided so that others can learn to operate a computer and still have their jobs. Your job will be to make sure you are giving them what they need to stay up with the current applications and programs.

Start-Up

Almost every one you know has a computer. That's really all you need to teach someone how to use the computer. If you don't have one in your home or the person don't have one in their home the public libraries are all over town and allow you to use their computers for free. Make up a contract with the person's information, how much you charge if you have a flat rate or charge by the hour. Leave a spot to indicate the place, day and times you will meet. Also generate a repayment if the person change their mind or if you have to cancel.

Suggestion:

Complete a couple of the free computer training classes at your local library. These is only if you need a guideline of what to teach. Advertise your services at local senior citizen homes, churches, shopping malls, coffee shops, places like that so that you can reach a population that is more likely to use your services.

Teaching computers is a wonderful way to make extra cash. All you really have to do is advertise, make sure you are targeting areas that will get you potential clients.

6.   Dating Service / Match Making

Now this can be a hard one but it is surely one of the best home based businesses out there. You have so many options with this. Online, matching making events, personals, the list goes on. Because the internet and chat lines are so hot you have to come up with a way to maximize your need. Why do people need you to find the love of their lives? What you have to first determine is rather you are going to be a multi functioning service or a specialized dating service. This can be very low in starting or extremely high depending on what you want to offer and how detailed you wont to be. (please do your research)

Start-Up
This will cost you as little as a couple hundred dollars to as much as a couple thousand. Don't let that scare you. Start off small with some local advertisement, make a personal data sheet. Go to other dating services and ask their prices. Get a feel of what is already being done and put your special touch on it.

Suggestion:
Rent a small hall and arrange a local singles night out. Have some refreshments, and games that people can play to get to know others in the room. Sale tickets to this event so that you know exactly how many people will be attending. With the sale if the tickets have a small questionnaire for the person to complete. At the night of the party have these questionnaire in a booklet so that others can go to a special area and browse them. If they find someone they would like to talk to you can set it up.

Use your imagination, be careful do some kind of back ground on the people you invite to your functions. There are free web search engines you can use or maybe you can invest in a yearly fee program used for people search.

7.   Desserts/Baking

Cakes and pies, cakes and pies mmmm mmmm good. Now this my friend is a step in the right direction. If you are a baker and can make a mouth watering moist cake, trust and believe you will be a thriving business in no time. People love to throw parties but can't seem to get the desserts just right so they stop at the local store and pick up a cake or pie, but when your name hit the fan they will be stopping at your home or waiting at their home with a smile for your delivery.

Start-Up
The same as catering if not less. If you are a baker you most likely have some equipment already. Pots, pans, stove and measuring utensils are your biggest overhead. You may need to get some larger pots and pans to handle larger orders. Search your local thrift shops. (my favorite goldmine)

If you do home made cakes and such be careful not to under price your things. You have to remember if you spend $10 for ingredients, what about your time and the heat to bake the items. Don't be afraid to ask for what you want. If your desserts are good there will be plenty of people making orders.

Suggestion:
Have a local bake sale at your church or at a social function. Set up a table and on each piece of dessert you sale have your card or a pamphlet with it, so people will know they can have more of your delicious baked goods at any time.

Do this every so often until you get your cliental where you like it.

You can get very creative with cakes. People like strange things. E-mail me I have some pictures of some crazy cakes.

<u>Remember desserts are not just cakes, but cookies, cobblers, candies, etc</u>

8.   Errand Service / Concierge

At the beginning you may not think this would be a great business to start, but if you do the right advertisement in the right area you will have an excellent chance to make lots of money. Corporate people can be a great start. They are too busy to do everything that needs to be done. The elderly is another great population to target. They need someone to take them out to the shopping store. See most people would just do it for them but your service will allow them to get out and socialize rather than just stay at home while everything is done for them. As you do more research you will be able to pin point what area you would like to serve.

Start-Up
One thing that would be of great use is an insured vehicle. If you don't have a car you would do a lot better at this business if you can get one. Try local pre-owned auto dealers.

Now that you have your car you are ready for business. Don't for get your contracts and business cards.

Suggestion:
The best thing here to do is put yourself out there. You have to get the word out that you are available. Ask if there is anything you can do for your friends, family, church members that they don't have time to do and charge a small fee. Once they have seen your dependability they will begin to spread the word and you will be off and running.

9.   Gambling Junkets

Rather you want to believe it or not this is a money making opportunity just waiting on you. While some people are spending more time worrying about where their next meal is, many others are worried about how they are getting to the casino. Now if you are provided a service for them to get there and return your outcome of cash will be endless. There are many services out here at are provided gambling junket trips. You can do only local or out of town trips. They can be for a few hours to a couple days. The choice is up to you.

Start-Up
Now this can be a bit up and down. You don't have to do the transporting. All you have to do is set the trips up and arrange for a local busing or transportation company to take you all there.

Making some flyers and business cards will be the start up. Call around to the local and surrounding casinos and ask for deals like free match plays, or lunch or dinner coupons. They are willing to offer you freebees to get you to come to their casino.

Make your traveler pre pay. Call some busing company to see what there prices are. This way you know what to charge per person for each trip.

Suggestion:
Rent a small school bus or passenger van and plan a one day trip to a surrounding casino. This will be your dry run so don't worry too much about profit. You have to get your feet wet. See what others are charging and be competitive but don't under charge. You wont to make money not give your away. t. This way you wont over spend. Offer some free drinks or snacks on the bus ride there. If you offer it they will come.

10.   Garage Sales

You can't go wrong with garage sales or sometimes known as yard sales, garage sales or rummage sales. People love to look over what others don't want. People can find great treasure with garage sales. If you are one that like to buy and resale you can make an unmentionable amount of money with yard sales. There is so much potential of success in this area. There are so many ways to go about this from using your back yard or garage on the weekends to local fairs and block sales. Remember one person's junk is another persons treasure.

Start-Up
Wow I cant think of a start up cost for this. You can start this with going through your own home and taking out things you are no longer using or call up friends and family to get you started. You can even offer your services to help clean up there attics or basements and you can take what they don't want any more. This will be a great way to get some merchandise for your 1st sale.

Suggestion:
Pick a weekend when you know there is more money in the community and set up shop in your front or back yard. Advertise by posting signs in your local grocery store and neighborhood stores.   Have some small post care sign flyer made to let your customers know when your next sale will be. Make sure each person that stops by get a flyer for your next sale. Have some balloons or colorful flags posted on your porch so that your house will be easy to notice. Sit back and watch your merchandise roll out and the bucks roll in.

11. Gift Baskets

You can become one of the neighborhood stars by arranging gift baskets. Everyone loves to give baskets for gifts, birthdays, anniversaries, baby showers, bridal showers you name it with a gift basket you can never go wrong. You can put your creative side to work. With most of the home based businesses listed in this booklet there are so many ways to go about doing your chosen area. You can have people bring their items to you and you arrange them in a beautiful basket for a small fee or you can purchase the items and make up baskets they can pick out but these baskets will have to be priced a bit higher than if they bring in their own items.

Start-Up
You will need to find some items on sale to have an array of merchandise to choose from. Ribbons, bows, baskets, stuffed animals, perfumes etc. This can become expensive. To start just pick a few styles that you can make up for displays or purchase. If you can invest about $200 to start you can get a good amount of products. Remember you are just starting out don't go for the high end baskets right away, unless you can afford it. However, if you can afford it by all means go for the gold.

Suggestion:
Make up a few baskets, 10 to 15 to start. Ask local stores or churches if you can place a table in or outside your location. As customer come in they will see what you have and purchase them. Always make sure you have business cards or flyer to give out. Also have a basket that you can give away as a raffle. Pre make some information tags asking for name, address, phone number so that you can notify them if they are the winner. This can be used to mail out information on your next sale or as advertising.

12.   Home Care / Elderly

I picked home care as one of the top 21 awesome home based businesses because there is a lot of money that can be made in this area. Let me say this though you have to do all your home work to get this going. You have to be very careful when working with health care. With the different things going on with Medicare and heath insurance, it is getting super hard to have the personal care that one really needs. This is where you come in. My advice here though is to stay away from the major health components of working with the elderly but become more of a companion. I say this because you are starting a small home based business and want to cut cost as much as possible. With providing home care you can still be a care worker but without the headaches of being sued for medication related issues and such. With your company you can offer just a step above elderly baby sitting. You can cook, watch the person take their meds and things like that and still get paid.

Start-Up
You need nothing to startup your cost can literally be $0 to start. Why you ask because all you need to do is put the word out that you are available to care for elderly people. Start with friends and family. If you have a car make sure you have insurance. Have a well defined service agreement the spells out what you will and will not do.

Suggestion:
Advertise in a few of your local neighborhood newspapers that you are an independent caregiver and that you are available. This way people will call you if they need your services. Make sure you let them know up front your prices and your limitations. This is very important to your business success. Don't let them talk you into doing what you are not comfortable with. RESEARCH

13. Jewelry Making

With today's economy people are finding it harder to keep up with the latest bling. This is where you will come in. You can use you creative flare and style to make some beautiful pieces. Use your creative side to open the eyes to fashion. You can use all styles from the African to American. People love things that shine. Throw in some silver and rhinestones people will eat it up.

Start-Up
Working with jewelry is going to be a bit prices at times. To start go with some simple pieces just o get your name out there. For $20 or $25 you can get a starter kit at your local Wal-mart store. They have loads of items to start you off. Prices range from $.99 and up. You can start with as much as you can afford to just get started.. As you make money you can always add more merchandise.

Oh yeah, if you can afford it start a web site, this will bring all kinds of income. Take pictures of your work and upload them to your site. Can you say Cha Ching? There are some sites you can get for free just do a Google search for free to low cost web hosting.

Suggestion:
After you have purchased your starter kit and other merchandise, make up at least 20 or so and host a jewelry make over party at your home. Invite your friends and family. Make sure you ask them to bring a friend along with them. Have some refreshment and display your jewelry. If you can afford it make some very inexpensive brackets tape them to a business card and give away to the first 5 or 10 people to come. If you don't sale all of your items that's ok just keep doing this over and over again. You will make the money.

14.   Party Planning

There are so many ways to use this talent. If you are one that can arrange parties and make them glamorous your talent will be sought out. People that like to host parties are not always sure of just what to do. You can come on as a consultant or arrange the party from start to finish. Do some research on what is going on in other city and town. You can even chose to just host local parties of your own and charge a fee for others to enjoy. Hook up with other people in your community that are doing things in this nature so that they can call on your expertise and vice a versa.

Start-Up

Off the bat all you need to do is advertise advertise advertise. Post in local bars, clubs and other places that you would think people would need your service. This can be a very successful business for you. Planning parties are weddings, events, singles, you name it. The possibilities are endless.

Suggestion:

Go to some local night clubs and ask if you can host a party at their establishment. What you have to do is make sure you will be able to charge a fee for entrance. You can even offer a small percentage of what you collect at the door. Make sure you have something to offer the party comers so that they would want to come. It could be drink specials, food, door prizes what ever you can come up with. Don't forget you are trying to make money not give yours away. Have a contest of some sort and let the other patrons be the judge. Have your business cards ready to give out so people know that you are ready to plan their next party.

15.   Pillow Designs

This can be a fun and personal home based business for you to consider. Many people like to decorate with pillows. It may be to add style to their living rooms, bedrooms or other areas of the house. You can specialize your designs for animals, prayer pillows, throw pillows or chair pillows. The possibilities are endless..

Start-Up
Your start up can be hard to determine. If you are going to do a number of pillows just to sale or if you are going to make pillows according to the request of your client. You will need to purchase many different fabrics and other frills to decorate your pillows. I would think you can start off with a couple hundred dollars to start. Needles, lace, paints, threads, and other material to decorate your many creations

Suggestion:
Prayer pillows are one of the hottest items around. You can make up a flyer and mail it to local churches in your area. Have samples to take pictures to add in your flyer. If you can post them on the internet that would be a great way to drum up business in there areas as well

Make sure you are not setting your prices too high that people cant afford to buy them but you have to also think about your material and time that you have put in making the pillows. A profit is what you are looking to make.

16.   Private Pay Child Care

Okay children lovers this can be the business of your dreams. With all the many state laws and classes you have to take to become a licenses childcare provider are getting way out of control. Classes are costing $50 and more. Being a private childcare provide will cut a lot of things you have to do. When you are being paid by a person out of their pocket you deal only with that person. There are no time sheets, classes or continuing education classes to take. Your care for your client's child is only between you and that person. Don't take on more that you can handle. Two or three children a week can bring in an extra $200 to $300 a week.

Start-Up

My favorite pass time is thrift shopping. You can spend all of $20 and get books and toys to share with the children you are caring for. Just make sure you clean them and keep them clean. Also purchase some extra snacks and allow the children to eat dinner or lunch with you until you start making money to buy special foods. You can chose to take care of the children in your home or your clients home.. Also you can take classes if you like to make a great portfolio for your clients so see.

Suggestion:

If you know of any one that has children and is paying for childcare out of pocket you can let then know that you are now in the business of childcare and you would love to provide care for their child. Ask them what they are paying now and give them a price brake so that you can be considered.

Again advertise in local paper or magazines that you are available for childcare. Give some prices ranges for different age groups. Let the people know that you are a specialty childcare that their child is your main concern. People that know you can also be a great way to speed the word.

17. Process Server

I thought about this home based business and the possibility of income can be great if it is done in the proper way. When you think about being a server there can be many concerns about the way you go about your job. If someone is being served more than likely they don't want to sign for any papers coming to them. You have to be creative in how you will serve papers. Do your research find out the persons work place, home or even relatives hone.. Chose times when you think the person will be home. Many people don't want to cause a scene on their jobs so they would be more willing to just sign for the papers.

Start-Up
All you will need to start this business a car to get to the person and the company that will be hiring you to so the work. If you don't currently have a vehicle it is recommended that you purchase or lease one before you begin work..

Suggestion:
Go through the yellow pages or do a web search on lawyers, property owners, or collection agencies. Design a letter introducing yourself and your new business. Let the person know what your fees are, when you will be available and what jobs you will not take on.

Before you start look into your state offices to make sure there is no special licenses or permits that you will need to do this service. Some states may required special licenses or permit. Protect yourself and make sure you are following all state, government and local laws.

18. Tax Preparation

Hey what can you say about tax preparation. This will be a great home base business. There are so many free or low cost internet services that you can use. These sites will figure out what the refunds or overdue payments will be. You only have to enter the information off the W2 forms.   This can a very lucrative business during tax time.

Start-Up
What you need to have is a computer and some time to spend entering your clients information. Depending on how intensive you would like to get into this business you might want to open a bank account in allow your clients payment to go there. This would give you the option of having your clients payment come out of their refund or for them to pay up front. Make sure you get all the correct information from the IRS that is would be allowed.

Suggestion:
Start by doing family and friends taxes and have them spread the word that you are now taking new clients for tax preparation. Advertise that you are doing taxes and half the cost of other tax preparers. This in itself will at least get the interest of people that have been pays $100s to have their taxes prepared.

With offering the bank deposit at the time of preparation gives you the option of letting your client know that their refunds will be coming sooner than if they chose to have it mailed. There is money to be made.

Don't forget make sure you are following all the rules and regulation for tax preparation.

19. Tutoring

Tutoring has been a great business for larger agencies. At some point children and even adults need to have someone show them how to bring up their skills in reading, math and other areas. You can charge a small free to work once or twice a week on homework help or on helping older adults that are looking to improve on their academic skills.

Start-Up
Here you may want to invest a few dollars to get things like early learning material. Books, pens, paper, and folders. You can shop at your local thrift shop and get some books that have been donated to start with. There you can find tons of material to use at all leaves.

Suggestion:
Ask some local schools if you can post an ad in there parent bulletin about your new services. Make sure you are telling them know exactly what areas you are going to be working with. You can also place ads in newspapers, community papers, and in other stores.

Visit some senior citizen homes or community centers. Here you can let the director know that you have a very inexpensive service for their clients. You may even want to set up a class where you can come to their center once a week and work with their clients.

Be very sensitive to your clients needs. Make sure you are allowing them to work at their own pace.

20.   Wake Up Service

"Good Morning this is your wake up call. Today is………..You will receive a call in 10 minutes as your final reminder its time to get up." That is a great way to start. Believe it or not some people still need to have that voice to get up from a nice sleep.   Now this may not be as lucrative as other mentioned home based businesses that are listed here, but if you are someone that cant get out and cant really afford to invest in starting another business at this time and are looking to make a few extra bucks here is a good way of starting out.

Start-Up
Advertise advertise advertise. Post in areas where you think people may need your service. If you can afford to take a small ad in your community newspaper do that. Craigslist and other internet posting agents can be great too.

All you need to have Is a working home phone or cell phone. Also make up a schedule so you can keep track of your clients and their call time.

Suggestion: You need to be extremely creative with this service. With alarm clocks and spouses people maybe reluctant to pay for someone to wake them up. If you can sing or can tell jokes use that in your advertisement to get their attention.

Remember don't be annoying or very loud when calling someone's home. Keep it tasteful and fun so that they will want to continue with your services. This will be for great at work conversations. You can hear them now, " I have this wake-up services and she is so hilarious or she has such a great singing voice. She gets me in a good mood for my day. You guys should try her."

21.   Web Designer

Cha-Cha-Ching!!!!!!!!!!!! Now this is a money making business. You can start out at home and chose to stay at home but with things today everyone wants a web site or web page. If you are good enough and can design web pages or sites you will be a great access to many people or businesses. You can arrange their information and also put your creative touch to make it stand out. This is a great way to being in that extra needed income.

Start-Up
It will be a great thing if you have your own computer and internet service at home. If you don't that will not be a problem. All local libraries allow people to use their computers and internet for free all you need is t have a current library card.

Design a service contract and let people know that you are out there. This can be a very competitive area but if your prices are right and your work is good people will use you.

Suggestion:
Design a webs site of your business. Add a couple pages of possible choices to allow possible clients to choose from. You can make these pages as detail or as simple as they like.

You can also make a PowerPoint presentation to take to appointments. You may even offer sample print outs from WebPages that you have designed. This will give the possible client an up front look at what you can do.

Now what are you going to do?

You have the last say.

Now I am sure that some of these Home Based Business cause for a little bit more researching. It is very important that you research any business that you are going to invest your time and money in. Don't just settle for what I have to say. You must get into your new business for yourself and let your gut feeling take you on what can be a great money making journey or a fly by night quick few bucks.

Good luck and may your endeavors

be prosperous.

If you chose to go with one of these home based business let me know what happened. I would love to know how things tuned out. Don't think because things are slow and the money is not coming as fast as you would like that your choice was the wrong choice. There is no written rule that only one business is for you.

If one of these highlighted business are not for you, let your talents take you to a place of endless possibilities. Maybe you have a skill or talent that is not listed here. Run with it, take a chance on yourself and see what can happen. If you spend a couple hundred bucks and only make a couple hundred then you are a winner because you tried. You and only you can make your dreams of becoming an entrepreneur come true.

I say go for it. Just keep me posted
fitness4life3@yahoo.com

**fitness4life
Helping you get
in shape for
your future**

**FYI:
In each suggestion area these suggestion can be used in all this business.**

If you need someone to communicate with while you get your home base business off the ground shoot me an e-mail.

fitness4life3@yahoo.com

This booklet was designed and published by Ailsa Stokes of Milwaukee, WI